Vol. 1

JUST WRITE THE SONG!

31 Songwriting Sessions & Prompts

Beat Writer's Block
& Create Beautiful Music

ALECIA RENECE

Copyright © 2019 by Alecia R. Harrison
All rights reserved. This book or any portion thereof may not be reproduced or used in any manner whatsoever without the express written permission of the publisher except for the use of brief quotations in a book review.
Printed in the United States of America
First Printing, 2019
Alecia Renece
www.aleciarenece.com

Dedicated to you.

I wrote this book with you in mind.
I created this book because I struggle with writer's block often and I figure that I couldn't be the only one. Perfectionism, self doubt, procrastination and lack of inspiration get in the way of me creating and writing my best music, and I wanted to do something about it. So I dedicate this book to you, fellow music maker.
You are talented. You are good enough. You are gifted. It's not a question of talent or ability.
Sometimes all we need is a little help to create our greatest work.

How To Use This Book

This book is broken up into "Sessions".

Each session contains a journaling exercise guided by a prompt.

After you complete your journal, you will be prompted to complete a brainstorming activity based on the journaling exercise to help you craft and get down ideas for your song.

There are many ways you can brainstorm.

Some people use word maps to write words, thoughts or ideas related to the topic of the session.

Some people prefer to use mind maps, 5W's (Who, What, Where, When, Why, [Sometimes How]) wordbanking… the list goes on and on…

The best way to brainstorm, is the easiest and quickest way for you. So choose a way and just go for it.

You don't want to waste too much time on brainstorming how you should brainstorm.

Don't allow procrastination to win!

You can complete each session on a schedule, or you can complete a session whenever you feel like it.

Though the choice is yours, I would recommend getting on some kind of schedule to best exercise your creative songwriting muscle.

You can do one session a day for 31 days or even once a week for 31 weeks.

Either way, keep showing up…

…When you don't feel like it.
…When you think it sucks.
…When you think the prompts are stupid.
…When you think the prompts are too hard.

Show up open and ready to give your art the time and dedication it needs to come to life.

Your songs don't have to be perfect, they just have to be.

If you're looking for community to journey with, be sure to join my free 5 Day Songwriting Challenge and Community at the link below:

https://www.aleciarenece.com/5-day-songwriting-challenge

Let's Begin.

Session One:

Close Your Eyes.
Think back on when you were a child.
What feelings, memories, scents, and traumas come to mind?
Write 5 below using words and/or complete thoughts.

Incorporate these thoughts and words into your song using this space below. Mind map, list, whatever you need to do to get ideas out for your song.

Song No. 1:

Date Completed:

Session 2:

Describe your morning routine.
Journal everything from the actual routines to your thoughts.
From waking up until you are ready to get going.
What are you eating? Are you smelling coffee? Is it cold?
Are you filled with hope? Despair? Dread? Excitement?
Let it all out below.

Brainstorm your song below (mind map, list, word lists, etc.)

Song No. 2:

Date Completed:

Session 3:

Who are you?
What are undeniable truths about you?
What is true about you no matter who you're with?
What do you believe? What are you made of? What are you passionate about?
What do you struggle with? What are you good at?
Who are you to other people? To yourself?

Brainstorm your song below.

Write a song using the prompt referring to yourself in the third person.

Song No. 3:

Date Completed:

Session 4:

Write a love letter to your best friend.
Say the things you're afraid to say.
Thank them.
Where did you meet?
What have you all been through?
What do they mean to you?
Where would you be without them?

Brainstorm your Song here.
Write a love letter in the form of a song for your best friend. Let them hear it.

Song No. 4:

Date Completed:

Session 5:

Write a love letter to yourself.
What do you need to hear right now?
You are the only You you'll ever have.
Cherish yourself.

Brainstorm your Song here.

Song No. 5:

Date Completed:

Session 6:

What is the advice you needed 10 years ago?
What have you learned since then?
How have you changed? Improved?
Someone needs that advice now.

Brainstorm your Song here.

Song No. 6:

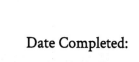

Session 7:

What do you see when you look in the mirror?
What is really there? Not what you want to see.
Wrinkles? Acne? Scars? A Smile? What shape? Form?
How did they get there?
What do you like? Dislike?
What have you come to accept?

You are a wonder.
Share the masterpiece that you are with us.
Brainstorm your song here.

Song No. 7:

Date Completed:

Session 8:

What do you hope to say looking back on your life 100 years from now?
What would you like to have accomplished?
What legacy, message and gift would you like to have left behind?
How do you want people to reflect on you and your life?

Life is for the living.
Live it.
Brainstorm Your Song Here:

Song No. 8:

Date Completed:

Session 9:

What is something you regret?
What do you wish you could take back?
What did it cost you?
What would you pay to get it back?

We all have regrets.
We're all working through them.
Begin to work through it here.

Song No. 9:

Date Completed:

Session 10:

What is your superpower?
How do you use it?
Do you conceal it in a secret identity?
Is it for good or evil?
Who/What/Where did you get it from?
What's your origin story?
How do you use it in the battle of good and evil?
Who/What is your weakness? Your arch nemesis?

We all are superheroes in our own ways.
The world needs you.

Song No. 10:

Date Completed:

Session 11:

Think about the first time you had your heart broken
Think about the last time you had it broken.
How does it really feel?
Does your chest crack open? A stone at the base of your throat? Is it hard to breathe?
Did you think you would die?
Are you currently working through heartache?
What hope do you hold onto?
What do you contemplate? What questions were left unanswered?
Do you want to give up?

Share that pain with those who need your story, here.

Song No. 11:

Date Completed:

Session 12:

What is your greatest fear?
List them out.
Get to the root of those fears and get to the root of those fears until you reach it.
Sit with it in silence.

Make that fear real for us here.

Song No. 12:

Date Completed:

Session 13:

Our parent(s).
They impact us whether we want to or not... for better and for worse.
Write a letter to them.
It can be grateful, angry, heartbreaking.
Just let it be honest.

Write it here.
Write a song communicating your truth.

Song No. 13:

Date Completed:

Session 14:

Go outside.
Take a walk with no music.
Take notes of what you see, hear, taste, feel, smell.
What feelings are invoked?
Annoyance, nostalgia, pain, joy?
Collect those notes below.

Write a song using your senses, referencing your feelings.

Song No. 14:

Date Completed:

Session 15:

Have a morning brain dump.
(I recommend doing this on a daily basis)
Just write non-stop for 7 minutes.
This should be a stream of consciousness.
If you can't think of anything, write that.
Just. Don't. Stop.

Take a break from your journal, then come back to re-read them.
Then, highlight or circle anything that resonates with or strikes you.
Use those lines in the beginning of your song or as a theme.
Begin writing based on those notes.

Song No. 15:

Date Completed:

Session 16:

Write a letter to The Fear your recognized in Session 12.

Are you angry at it? Understanding? Forgiving?
What have you always wanted to say to it?
Let your fear know exactly how you feel.

Be honest. It's Freeing.

Song No. 16:

Date Completed:

Session 17:

Life can be a struggle.
What are some of your daily struggles?
Is it getting out of bed? Getting to sleep?
Rush hour traffic? Gigging? Showing up for your art?
List a few struggles below.

Pick a few struggles to reference and build a song around below.

This can *totally* be a vent session.

Song No. 17:

Date Completed:

Session 18:

Imagine your life is a TV show.
Is it a comedy? Drama? Reality Show?
Who are your main characters?
Every show needs a theme song.
What would be yours?
Theme songs are usually no more than 30 seconds long.
It's long enough to share what the show is about, set the mood and introduce the main characters.

Brainstorm your show and Jingle below.

Song No. 18:

Date Completed:

Session 19:

What is you favorite time of the day?
Why is that?
What does it feel like? Look like? Sound like? Taste and smell like, even?
What internal feelings does this time of day invoke?
What is the process of getting to this time of day?
Who do you see, if anyone?

Paint that picture for us.

Song No. 19:

Date Completed:

Session 20:

Sweet sounds.
What comes to mind when you hear that word?
What are some of the sweetest sounds you've ever heard?
Is it a baby laughing? Birds chirping after a heart-broken night?
List some of your favorites below.
Describe those sounds in great detail.

Share those sounds with us as though we were there with you listening along.

Song No. 20:

Date Completed:

Session 21:

What is a song you really love right now?
Why?
Is it the chords? The lyrics? The cadence?
Use the parts you love about that song as a base for your own song.
If it's the chord progression, write to that.
If it's a lyric that really knocks you in the chest, start your song with that line.

The goal isn't to plagiarize, but to be inspired by what moves you. Share those pieces with us.

Song No. 21:

Date Completed:

Session 22:

Four Seasons for some. Two Seasons for others.
What is your favorite season?
What do you love most about it?
Using your 6 senses, describe that season to us as if we've never experienced it.
We really haven't. Not like you have.
For added challenge, what kind of person or animal would the Season be?
What would be their characteristics, dreams, pet peeves, etc.
Make them real to us.

Share your season with us.

Song No. 22:

Date Completed:

Session 23:

You have seen you for most everyday of your life, yet it can be difficult to describe yourself to others.
Stand in the mirror for 5 minutes, really taking in your masterpiece of a body.
Try to write down some descriptives when it comes to your face.
Your descriptions don't have to be literal.
They should also be what you think of yourself, not what others think.
We tend to adopt insecurities and descriptions other people give to us, and forget what we think of ourselves.
What does it feel like to be in your skin?
What does your skin feel like? Your eyes really look like?

We want to know the real you.
Share with us.

Song No. 23:

Date Completed:

Session 24:

How does sunlight feel?
What about Moonlight?
How do they relate to one another?
Do they know of each other?
How do you act in the sun and the moon? Why are they different?
Do you prefer one over the other?

Let us know your thoughts.

Song No. 24:

Date Completed:

Session 25:

Who is You at 100%?
What are your flaws? Your strengths? Your secret pleasures?
Where is a place that you can be 100% yourself?
Describe that place to us.
Is anyone there? If so, who?
If not, why?
Describe it to us using your 6 senses.

Let us into your sanctuary.

Song No. 25:

Date Completed:

Session 26:

Sometimes pieces of ourselves can be broken up or shared over multiple places at once.
We can willingly and lovingly give our loved ones a piece of our hearts.
Sometimes it can feel like a piece of us has been bitterly and jaggedly broken off through a break-up, move, death or fall-out.
Where are these places for you?
Describe them to us.
Can you ever get them back?
What do they feel like?
Who is there? Who isn't?
Who is missing?

Let us touch and pick up those pieces.

Song No. 26:

Date Completed:

Session 27:

What is something you need to get rid of that you haven't yet?
Why haven't you?
What is it?
Is it a person, mindset, belonging?
What would it mean for you to let that go?
Is it difficult? Why?

Let. It. Go. Here.

Song No. 27:

Date Completed:

Session 28:

What does it mean to be grateful?
What does it look like, sound like for you?
What are some things you're thankful for today?
List at least 25 things you can be grateful for.
It can be "big" or "small".
Just list it.

Share a song highlighting at least 5 of the things on your list.

Song No. 28:

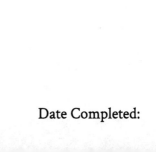

Session 29:

What is your favorite color?
Why?
Describe it without saying "it".
What does it feel like?
How does it sound?
How does it make you feel?
If it had a personality, what would be its attributes?

Describe it for us through song.

Song No. 29:

Date Completed:

Session 30:

Every hometown needs an anthem.
Where is your hometown?
What do you remember about it?
What stands out that sets it apart from anywhere you've gone?
How has it made you who you are today?
Were there any frustrations from your hometown?
What do you love about it?

Describe it to use as if we've never been there.
Use your 6 senses.
Make it feel like home to us.

Song No. 30:

Date Completed:

Session 31:

What is your life's mission statement at this point in your life?
List your core values.
List your beliefs.
What legacy would you like to leave behind?
How would you like for your life to impact others?
What would be the indicator that you lived a fulfilling life?

Let us know your mission statement through song.

Song No. 31:

Date Completed:

Congratulations, Friend!

You did it.
I am so proud of you.
You should be proud of yourself.

Now, why don't you share your music with the world?

If this was helpful to you, join our free 5 day songwriting challenge where you can continue to make great music and build community in the process.

Sign up at
https://www.aleciarenece.com/5-day-songwriting-challenge

Alecia Renece is a soul singer-songwriter, storyteller and multi-passionate artist who uses her life's heartbreaks and triumphs as fuel to create authentic and honest art to share with others.

When she's not taking photos, making music or writing, she can be found having fun with her husband, hanging with friends and family, reading a book, eating and dreaming.

For more information, visit her at www.aleciarenece.com.

Made in the USA
Columbia, SC
09 March 2021